CW00499831

# 1 MONTH OF
# FREE
# READING

at

**www.ForgottenBooks.com**

By purchasing this book you are eligible for one month membership to ForgottenBooks.com, giving you unlimited access to our entire collection of over 1,000,000 titles via our web site and mobile apps.

To claim your free month visit:

www.forgottenbooks.com/free743914

* Offer is valid for 45 days from date of purchase. Terms and conditions apply.

ISBN 978-0-483-61536-6
PIBN 10743914

This book is a reproduction of an important historical work. Forgotten Books uses state-of-the-art technology to digitally reconstruct the work, preserving the original format whilst repairing imperfections present in the aged copy. In rare cases, an imperfection in the original, such as a blemish or missing page, may be replicated in our edition. We do, however, repair the vast majority of imperfections successfully; any imperfections that remain are intentionally left to preserve the state of such historical works.

Forgotten Books is a registered trademark of FB &c Ltd.
Copyright © 2018 FB &c Ltd.
FB &c Ltd, Dalton House, 60 Windsor Avenue, London, SW19 2RR.
Company number 08720141. Registered in England and Wales.

For support please visit www.forgottenbooks.com

Terms—One Dollar a Year.

# THE
# RICAN REPOSITORY.

XXVI. JULY, 1860 No. 7.

## CONTENTS.



Published Monthly by the American Colonization Society.

WASHINGTON:
C. ALEXANDER, PRINTER,
NEAR WAR AND NAVY DEPARTMENTS.

GE—To any part of the United States, *six cents* a year, if paid
quarterly or yearly in advance.

## Officers of the American Colonization Society.

---

*President:*

JOHN H. B. LATROBE, Esq.

*Corresponding Secretary:*

Rev. R. R. GURLEY.

*Financial Secretary and Treasurer:*

Rev. WILLIAM McLAIN.

*Travelling Secretary:*

Rev. JOHN ORCUTT.

*Executive Committee:*

HARVEY LINDSLY, M. D.,
JOSEPH H. BRADLEY, Esq.,
WILLIAM GUNTON, Esq.,
Rev. GEORGE W. SAMSON, D. D.,
Hon. WILLIAM M. MERRICK,
Hon. GEORGE P. SCARBURGH.
Hon. PETER PARKER.

# THE AFRICAN REPOSITORY.

Vol. XXXVI.] WASHINGTON, JULY, 1860. [No. 7.


## The Foreign Slave Trade;

### CAN IT BE REVIVED WITHOUT VIOLATING THE MOST SACRED PRINCIPLES OF HONOR, HUMANITY, AND RELIGION?

WE are indebted for this able pamphlet (which first appeared in the Southern Presbyterian Review) to the Rev. J. LEIGHTON WILSON, D. D., for many years a Missionary in Africa, and now Secretary of the Presbyterian Board of Foreign Missions.

Mr. Wilson is a native of South Carolina; writes not only from careful examination of the reports of travellers, but from much personal observation on the subject, and with those earnest convictions of duty which true religion cannot fail to produce. Those who peruse this pamphlet will see clearly, that the abolition of this trade is essential to the civilization of Africa.

Mr. Wilson is led to believe that "the Slave Trade has always been attended with scenes of the greatest cruelty, and that almost all the anarchy, misery, bloodshed and warfare that have reigned in that country, for two centuries past, are to be traced to this source."

If there be one prayer which should at this time be daily on the lips of all Christians, it is this, "From hardness of heart, from blindness of mind, and from contempt of Thy Word and Commandments, good Lord deliver us!" Evil passions by indulgence may increase without limit, so that the victims of them come finally to put darkness for light and light for darkness. They wander in desolate places like dead men, and know not at what they stumble. Destruction and misery are in their paths, and the way of peace they know not.

When Granville Sharp and Clarkson girded themselves with strength to expose the horrors of this worst of piracies, the African Slave Trade, the hearts of all civilized nations were moved with sorrow and compassion, and the eloquence of the greatest statesmen was never silent until law denounced it as a crime against human nature. Will they be required to do over again what they then did so well? Must the immortal words they wrote and spoke, the irresistible arguments they urged, their fearful descriptions and pathetic appeals, be reproduced to touch and subdue the hearts of the present generation? We proceed to give a large part of Mr. Wilson's pamphlet:

"We begin our quotations from Bruce, the well known traveller in Abyssinia and Eastern Africa. In speaking of the slave-hunts in those regions, he says:

"The grown-up men are all killed, and are then mutilated, parts of their bodies being always carried away as trophies; several of the old mothers are also killed, while others, frantic with fear and despair, kill themselves. The boys and girls of a more tender age are then carried off in brutal triumph."

Major Denham, who travelled through the greater part of Soudan in 1823, gives the following account of the miseries entailed upon that part of the country by the prosecution of this traffic. Speaking of the slave-hunts, several of which he witnessed with his own eyes, he writes:

"On attacking a place, it is the custom of the country instantly to fire it; and, as they (the villages) are all composed of straw huts only, the whole is shortly devoured by the flames. The unfortunate inhabitants fly quickly from the devouring element, and fall immediately into the hands of their no less merciless enemies, who surround the place; the men are quickly massacred, and the women and children lashed together and made slaves."

He adds, in the same connection, that the Begharmi nation had been defeated by the Sheik of Bornou in five successive expeditions, in which not less than 20,000 men were slaughtered, and not less than 15,000 more were reduced to slavery. He gives the following account of a treaty of alliance between the Sheik of Bornou and the Sultan of Mandara:

"This treaty of alliance was confirmed by the Sheik's receiving in marriage the daughter of the Sultan, and the marriage portion was to be the produce of an immediate expedition into the Kerdy country, by the united forces of these allies. The results were as favorable as the most savage confederacy could have anticipated. Three thousand unfortunate wretches were dragged from their native wilds, and sold to perpetual slavery, while probably *double that number were sacrificed to obtain them.*"

He mentions the following fact as having occurred under his own eyes: "Darkala was quickly burnt, and another small town near to it, and the few inhabitants found in them, chiefly infants and aged persons, were put to death without mercy, and thrown into the flames."

Ashmun, the well-known philanthropist, and formerly Governor of Liberia, communicated the following statement to the Colonization Society in 1823:

"The following incident I relate, not for its singularity, for similar events take place, perhaps, every month in the year; but it has fallen under my own observation, and I can vouch for its authenticity: King Boatswain, our most powerful supporter, and steady friend among the natives (so he has uniformly shown himself), received a quantity of goods on trust from a French slaver, for which he stipulated to pay young slaves—he makes it a point of honor to be punctual to his engagements. The time was at hand when he expected the return of the slaver, and he had not the slaves. Looking around on the peaceable tribes about him for his victims, he singled out the Queahs, a small agricultural and trading people of most inoffensive character. His warriors were skilfully distributed to the different hamlets, and making a simultaneous assault upon the sleeping occupants in the dead of the night, accomplished, without difficulty or resistance, in one hour, the annihilation of the whole tribe—every adult, man and woman, was murdered—every hut fired! Very young children, generally, shared the fate of their parents; the boys and girls alone were reserved to pay the Frenchman."

The following statement is contained in an official report made by the mixed Commission Court at Sierra Leone, to the British Government, in 1825:

"The Cassoos are represented as having carried fire, rapine and murder throughout the different villages through which they passed, most of the women and children of which, together with the prisoners, were immediately sold to the slavefactors, who were at hand to receive them."

Lander, with whose travels, adventures, and discoveries, almost every school-boy is familiar, makes the following statements about this traffic:

"It has produced the most baleful effects, causing anarchy, injustice, and oppression to reign in Africa, and exciting nation to rise up against nation, and man against man; it has covered the face of the country with desolation. All these evils, and many others, has slavery accomplished: in return for which, the Europeans, for whose benefit, and by whose connivance and encouragement, it has flourished so extensively, have given to the heartless natives ardent spirits, tawdry silk dresses, and paltry necklaces of beads."

McGregor Laird, Esq., a gentleman well known in Liverpool at the present day, and the chief contractor of the steam mail line between England and the west coast of Africa, ascended the Niger, in 1832, to the confluence, and gives the following account of the proceedings of the Felatahs, a well-known Mohammedan tribe, who are constantly engaged in capturing slaves to be transported to the sea-coast. He writes:

"Scarcely a night passed but we heard the screams of some unfortunate beings that were carried off into slavery by these villainous depredators. The inhabitants of the towns in the route of the Felatahs fled across the river on the approach of the enemy." "A few days after the arrival of the fugitives, a column of smoke rising in the air, about five miles above the confluence, marked the advance of the Felatahs; and, in two days afterwards, the whole of the towns, including Addah, Cuddah, and five or six others, were in a blaze. The shrieks of the unfortunate wretches that had not escaped, answered by the loud wailings and lamentations of their friends and relations (encamped on the opposite bank of the river), at seeing them carried off into slavery, and their habitations destroyed, produced a scene which, though *common enough in the country*, had seldom, if ever before, been witnessed by European eyes, and showed to me, in a more striking light than I had hitherto beheld it, the horrors attendant upon this traffic."

Col. Nichols, formerly Governor of Fernando Po, states, in a letter to Mr. Buxton, in relation to a visit which he made to Old Calabar in 1834, that "he found the natives boasting of a predatory excursion, in which they had recently been engaged, in which they had surprised a village, killed those who had resisted, and carried off the remainder as slaves. I heard an African boy, who formed one of the party, declare that he had killed three himself."

Rev. Mr. Fox, a well-known Wesleyan missionary at the Gambia, and the author of a most excellent volume on that part of the country, makes the following statement, in a communication to the Board of Missions in 1837:

"The neighborhood of McCarthy's Island is again in a disturbed state. Scarcely are the rains over, and the produce of a plentiful harvest gathered in, ere the noise of battle and the din of warfare is heard at a distance, with all its attendant horrors. Mothers, snatching up their children, with a few necessary articles, flee for their lives; towns, after being pillaged of as much cattle, etc., as the banditti require, are immediately set on fire; columns of smoke ascend the heavens; the cries of those who are being butchered may be more easily conceived than expressed; and those who escape destruction are carried into the miseries of hopeless slavery. A number of Bambarras are again on the north bank of the river, not far from this place, and the poor Foulahs at Jamalli have consequently fled to this island for protection, bringing with them as many of their cattle, and other things, as they could."

Rev. Mr. McBrair, another missionary, of the same place and connection, and the author of several valuable volumes on African languages, in a letter to the Secretary of the Wesleyan Society of about the same date, states:

"On other occasions, a party of men-hunters associate together, and falling suddenly upon a small town or village during the night, they massacre all the men that offer any resistance, and carry away the rest of the inhabitants as the best parts of their spoil. Or, when a chieftain thinks himself sufficiently powerful, he makes the most frivolous excuses for waging war upon his neighbors, so that he may spoil his country of its inhabitants." He learned, further, "that the wholesale method of seizure is, by far, the most frequent, and that, without this plan, a sufficient number of victims could not be obtained for the market; so that it may be called the prevailing way of obtaining slaves."

Mr. Morgan, another missionary of the highest respectability in the same region of country, writes:

"I feel confident that the slave-trade has established feuds among the African tribes about the Gambia, by which they will be embroiled in war for generations to come, unless the disposition be destroyed by Christianity, or their circumstances be changed by civilization."

John Duncan, Esq., under the auspices of the Royal Geographical Society, penetrated to the Kong Mountains in 1847, by passing through the country of Dahomy, one of the chief seats of the foreign slave-trade even down to the present day, and makes the following remarks about the terrible desolations caused in that region of country by the slave-hunts. He writes:

"But the horrors of the slave-trade commence when the king of any country is in want of slaves. Some pretence is got up for making war, although it is nothing more than a slave-hunt. This is conducted in the following manner:

The point of attack is probably reconnoitered by one individual during the day, who then retires, most likely unsuspected of any evil design. The attacking party is afterwards marched close to the town, and, about two hours before day-break, an impetuous rush is made upon the place, which (in the interior) is generally surrounded by a broad, close-growing fence of dangerous prickly bushes, about fifteen feet high. Such, however, is the practice and dexterity of the King of Dahomy's female soldiers, that this terrible fence is scarcely deemed an obstacle. Then commences the dreadful capture and slaughter. The people, in general, are asleep when the attack is begun, and, when roused so suddenly—and, perhaps, their house already on fire—make some resistance, whereupon they are instantly put to death. The others are tied around the neck with a piece of small grass-rope, each soldier having that article, as well as a piece of chalk. Each soldier uses his own private mark on the back of as many slaves as he may capture, and also secures the scalps of as many as he may kill in the attack. After all is over, these slaves and scalps are presented to the chief, who gives each soldier an amount of cowries proportioned to the number of captives he has taken, and also allows him to attach an additional cowry to the stock of his gun, which is accounted a mark of honorable distinction."

Rev. T. J. Bowen, a native of Georgia, and a missionary of the Southern Baptist Board, in Western Africa, in a volume of travels recently published, and with which many of the readers of this article are undoubtedly already familiar, makes the following statements about the effects of the slave-trade upon Yoruba, the scene of his own missionary labors: "I have counted the sites of eighteen desolated towns within a distance of sixty miles between Badagry and Abeokuta, the legitimate result of the slave-trade. The whole of Yoruba is full of depopulated towns, some of which were even larger than Abeokuta at the present time. And yet Abeokuta is supposed to contain, at the present time, more than 100,000 inhabitants. Of all the places visited by the Landers, only Ishaki, Igboho, Ikishi, and a few other villages remain. Ijenna was destroyed a few weeks after my arrival in the country. Other and still larger towns in the same region have recently fallen. At one, called Oke Oddan, the Dahomy army captured and killed about 20,000, on which occasion the king presented Domingo, the Brazilian slaver, with 600 slaves. The whole number of people destroyed in this section of country within the last fifty years, cannot be less than 500,000!!!" Mr. Bowen may well say, as he does in the same connection: "Well-meaning people who advocate the restoration of the slave-trade, have considered but one side of the question."

The last authority I would quote is that of the celebrated German traveller, Dr. Barth, who, it is well known, has just returned from one of the most thorough and extensive explorations ever made in Central Africa, and whose statements will be received with entire confidence in all parts of the civilized world. He represents those interior regions as in the same disturbed and unhappy condition that they were in the days of Clapperton and Denham; and assigns the same cause for their unhappiness and distraction. He accompanied the Sheik of Bornou on one of his slave-hunts, as Major Denham had done more than thirty years ago." Some of the scenes witnessed on this excursion were truly heart-sickening. He says:

"The village we had just reached was Kahala, and is one of the most considerable places in the Musgu country. A large number of slaves had been caught this day: and in the course of the evening, after some skirmishing, in which three Bornou horsemen were killed, a great many more were killed; altogether, there were said to be a thousand, and there were certainly not less than five hundred. To our utmost horror not less than one hundred and seventy full-grown men were mercilessly slaughtered in cold blood, the greater part of them being allowed to bleed to death, a leg having been severed from the body."

On another occasion, he says:

"The whole village, which, only a few moments before, had been the abode of comfort and happiness, was destroyed by fire, and made desolate. Slaughtered men, with their limbs severed from their bodies, were lying about in all directions, and made the passer-by shudder with horror."

Any amount of similar testimony might be brought together if it were necessary. It is not in the capture of slaves alone, however, that these cruelties are practised. Equally as great harshness is inflicted on their journey to the sea-coast, during their detention there, and on what is called the middle passage, which, in fact, is but another term for the grossest cruelties ever practised upon any portion of the human race. We might speak of the principal highways to the sea-coast as strewed with human bones, of human limbs worn to the bone with iron fetters, of hundreds of these human beings starved to death in the barracoons, because no vessel came to take them away at the appointed time; or of whole cargoes suffocated to death in the hold of the ship by the attempt to avoid detection; but we refrain from these painful details. After a most careful examination of this whole subject, extending our inquiries over a period of more than a hundred years, and carefully weighing the statements of more than fifty different authors, we have come to the deliberate conclusion that, in the seizure of slaves, in the march to the sea-coast, during their detention there, and on the middle passage, the destruction of life must be more than one hundred and fifty per cent. upon those safely landed in America—so that to get one hundred slaves for practical purposes, at least one hundred and fifty lives must be sacrificed! Let us dwell upon this startling fact. In order to procure 100,000 laborers for the cotton and sugar-fields of the South, we must go into the business with the full understanding that it cannot be done except by sacrificing the lives of at least 150,000 immortal beings, to say nothing of the wide-spread desolation which it must occasion in other respects in Africa. Is the South prepared for this? Will she forego her honor, her sense of justice, and her religion, so far as to associate herself with the vilest men that have ever disgraced the annals of humanity, and once more apply the torch of discord and war for the purpose of obtaining slaves? Can American civilization be promoted in no other way than by trampling out the last spark of life from the continent of Africa? Has the Creator no other object in forming this great continent, and filling it with inhabitants, than that it should become the theatre for the display of the worst passions of the rest of the world?

If any one would have a true picture of the cruel and desolating results that follow in the train of the slave-trade, especially in those portions of the country we have under more special review at the present moment, let him peruse the pages of Barth with care and patience; note down the almost innumerable sites of desolated towns and cities through which he passed; the diminished population of the country, compared with what it was thirty years ago when visited by Denham, and let him observe, above all, the perpetual strifes and exterminating wars going on in what would otherwise be one of the most peaceful and prosperous portions of that whole continent. Nor has this traffic been less disastrous to the great Pagan kingdoms nearer the sea-coast. Benin and Congo have become completely disorganized, and neither, at the present day, can put up a plausible claim to a distinctive nationality. They retain now nothing but the name of their former greatness. Yoruba would have reached the same condition, if it had not been for the timely change in the tide of affairs, consequent upon the return of so many of her children from Sierra Leone, with the blessings of civilization and Christianity in their hands. Dahomy was once proud of her military prowess, and could count her population by hundreds of thousands, but is now rapidly sinking to the condition of mere lawless banditti. Ashanti, with her 2,000,000 of inhabitants, would, long ere this, have reached the same condition of anarchy and depopulation, if her slave-trade had not been arrested by the operation of the British forts along the Gold Coast.

We do not ascribe all this disorder and deterioration to the exclusive influence of the slave-trade. Africa is essentially a heathen country, and heathenism every where combines in itself almost every element of moral and social evil. But the slave-trade has quickened and given intensity to all these elements of discord, and has thus made the the African race one of the most unhappy and miserable people on the face of the earth.

Thus far our remarks have been restricted to the influence of the slave-trade upon those portions of the country where it has been carried on by open warfare, and upon what may be denominated the wholesale operation. We proceed now to speak of its influence upon other parts of the country, where it has assumed the outward form of a peaceful commerce; and we shall endeavor to show that, notwithstanding this more favorable exterior, it has not been less destructive of the peace and welfare of the country than the other system. On the previous part of our subject, we have been compelled to rely, in a great measure, upon the testimony of others. In what is to follow, we shall speak only of what we know, and testify only to what we have seen.

That portion of the population of Western Africa, of which we are now to speak, though comprising only the smaller tribes or communities, forms, nevertheless, the great mass of the population of the country; and it is from this class that the great body of the slaves have heretofore been obtained. The principal points along the sea-coast where this traffic was formerly concentrated were at or near the mouths of the rivers Pongas, Gallinas, Sestos, Asaini, Poppo, Lagos, Benin, and Bonny, in Upper Guinea; and at Old Calabar, Cameroons, Gaboon, Cape Lopez, Mayumba, Loango, Congo, Loando, and Benguela, in Lower Guinea. So long as there was no prohibition of the traffic, vessels were in the habit of collecting their cargoes by touching at all or most of these points, and purchasing such slaves as might happen to be on hand. Sometimes a cargo was obtained by robbing some other vessel that had collected one, but which happened to be without the means of defence. The trade has always been characterized by piratical proceedings, and would, no doubt, be so in all future times, even if it were legalized. * *

Mr. Wilson shows that, since the coast has been guarded by squadrons, factories and barracoons have been established at different points, in which slaves may be gradually collected, to await the coming of the slave ship, to which they can be clandestinely, and in a few hours, transferred. But how are these slaves obtained for market? With few exceptions, Mr. Wilson states, "they are not persons who were born in a state of servitude. We know that an African slave dealer would almost as soon sell his own son as a bond slave born in his own house."

Persons are doomed to foreign servitude in Africa for various causes, and in a variety of ways. In the great majority of cases it is professedly for crimes or misdemeanors. Murder is always punished in this way, if a slave-factory is within reach. Theft and adultery, although ordinarily doing no great violence to the moral sense of the people, are sure to be magnified into crimes of the deepest dye, if there is any possibility of selling the offender. A refractory wife, if suspected of infidelity to her husband, is very apt to be hurried away to a slave-factory before the blood-relations can possibly interfere in her behalf.

The most prolific source of all, however, is to be found in the charge of witchcraft. This superstition has an existence in Africa farther back, and entirely independent of the slave-trade; and none but those who have been initiated into the mysteries of African life can form any right conception of the absolute authority which it exercises over that race. The belief in it is one of the first, the deepest, and most enduring of all the impressions made upon their childhood. It grows with the growth of every man and woman in the land, and finds something to strengthen its hold upon the popular feeling in every day's experience and observation. It insinuates itself into the usages, the laws, the religion, and indeed into the entire fabric of the moral and social system. It undermines all the deep foundations of society, and keeps every family and community in a state of uneasiness and perturbation. No worse suspicion can possibly affix itself to any man's character. It breaks in twain the strongest bonds that hold human society together. The child is discharged from all filial duty, and the father or mother from all parental obligation, if the slightest taint of this suspicion rests upon the character of either. The brother will denounce the sister, or the sister the brother, if either falls under the condemnation of public opinion. The husband will thrust from his bosom the most cherished wife, if she does not, upon the first insinuation of a suspicion, purge her character by a resort to some of the appointed tests of witchcraft. Hundreds and thousands of innocent men and women are annually put to death in Africa in obedience to the demands of this foul demon.

If the slave-trader could get to the rescue of this class of persons, and confine his operations to them alone, then indeed his calling would be one of mercy. But, unfortunately, his presence and avocation but add fuel to the flame. Direful as are the fruits of this insane superstition, they are rendered tenfold more so under the stimulation of this cruel traffic. Under its influence the charge of witchcraft is multiplied a hundred-fold, and when the work of crimination and recrimination is fairly started in any community, it produces a state of society that scarcely has any parallel, and can neither be described nor understood. Old grudges are started into life, and every possible means is employed to obtain revenge through the medium of this subtle agency. Avarice comes forth in all her might, and hesitates not to ally herself with this all-pervading superstition for the accomplishment of her purposes. The defenceless stranger, under the sanction of her authority, is seized upon and hurried away to the slave-factory, never to see his home or his kindred again. The silent traveller is suddenly seized by men who have waylaid his path, and after a hurried and mock trial, finds himself in the hands of a white man—the representative of the Christian world—who listens to no protestations of innocence, and knows not how to relax his grasp. The unfortunate wife, who has incurred the displeasure of her lord, is accused of this great crime, and, without the formality of a trial, is handed over to the slave-trader, and thus doomed to perpetual servitude in a foreign land. A family burdened with the care of a feeble or idiotic member, will countenance the charge of witchcraft against him by others, for the twofold object of sharing in the profits of his sale, and getting rid of the care and expense of a burdensome member. A man who has excited the cupidity or the envy of his fellow-men by his superior wealth is liable to be brought under condemnation, and be sent abroad, from nothing but a desire for plunder on the part of others. Of course these acts of cruel injustice do not go unrevenged. Those who bring about the downfall of others, through mere motives of envy or cupidity, must expect to reap the bitter fruits of their own sowing. The friends of the stranger, who has been so unceremoniously bartered away, will seek revenge by murdering the chief actor in the affair, or some townsman, and thus throw the whole responsibility on the original offender. And when these deeds of retaliation commence, no one can tell where they will end. I have myself heard the midnight discharge of eight or ten muskets in the same neighborhood, each of which told of a slain victim, and all to revenge the sale of a single individual to a slave-factory the day before. Indeed, the very presence of a slave-factory in any community is but the sign and symbol of perpetual disturbance and petty warfare. Jealousy and distrust reign in every heart, and no one feels secure of life and limb. No man lies down to sleep without planting a loaded musket at the head of his bed. The silence of the night is constantly disturbed by screams that are intended to frighten away lurking enemies. No man will venture fifty rods from his own door during such periods of excitement, without being armed. The women of any town may not venture to the common watering-place, or visit their little farms for the purpose of getting the fruits of their previous labors, without being accompanied by an armed escort. The sound of a distant oar, or the rustling of a banyan leaf, will cause a panic of fear, and throw a whole community into the utmost perturbation.

But this disturbed state of society, and these acts of perpetual violence, are scarcely more to be deprecated than the moral insensibility that is engendered by the traffic. Cases do occur, though we are glad for the sake of humanity that they are not very frequent, where parents have consented to the sale of their own children. The other relationships of life are less regarded. I have known two young men from a distant part of the country, professed friends, to visit the neighborhood of a slave-factory for the purpose of curiosity, or for general observation, when one has secretly bartered away the other, and gone home and divided the proceeds of his sale with his own friends. It is not uncommon in the history of this business for a man to find himself in the same barracoon along by the side of individuals whom he himself had sold there only a few days or weeks previously. I have known a company of six or eight men, at the beginning, sworn friends, who have successively conspired against each other, and in almost every case on the charge of witchcraft, until the last man was sold by some one else, and the whole company carried away in the same cargo. And this state of insensibility and treachery, let it be remembered is brought about among a people who are naturally kind, affectionate, and confiding, and who would live in peace and comparative happiness, if it were not for the disturbing element we have under consideration.

There are great wrongs and injuries also inflicted upon these people during their imprisonment on the sea-coast. The owner of the factory intends to be kind to the slaves he has purchased. It is his interest to provide wholesome food, and use all the means the circumstances of the case will allow, to preserve their lives and health. But, unfortunately, he partakes of the insensibility that his avocation almost always produces. Any murmuring or attempt to escape on the part of his imprisoned subjects is very apt to be punished with instant death—yes! death inflicted without even the formality of a trial, and under circumstances sometimes of great cruelty. Sickness, too, often makes great havoc in the ranks of these unfortunate beings. No sooner does death take place (and in many cases even before life is extinct) than the miserable victim is dragged out in the open field to putrify or to be devoured by beasts. I have myself walked over fields that were strewed with the bones of those who had been thrown out of these factories. There is, or was, a few years ago, on the island of Corisco, a mound of human bones, that were gathered there from a neighboring slave-factory, and no doubt many were laid on that pile before the light of reason, or the breath of life, had been extinguished. This is a painful picture, but no more painful than true, and it ought to be attentively considered by those who advocate the revival of this wicked traffic. * * * *

Now, we would ask, is it possible for honorable, Christian men to lend their countenance to such business? Will the high-minded men of the South consent to obtain laborers for their plantations on such terms? —Are there no other ways by which an honorable living may be obtained? Shall we, knowingly and deliberately, sanction all the marauding, pillaging, kidnapping, and murdering that are inseparably connected with the traffic? What, though Northern merchants are ready to advance their money and employ their ships in the traffic, does this alter the true complexion of the affair? Can the prosperity of the South be promoted in no other way than by reducing the continent of Africa to a scene of perpetual tumult and warfare?

## Letter of Mr. Ralston to Lord Brougham.

Gerard Ralston, Esq., Consul General of Liberia in London, has addressed the following letter to Lord Brougham. Mr. Ralston is a citizen of the United States, though for several years a resident of London, and like his venerable father, the late Robert Ralston, of Philadelphia, distinguished both for patriotism and philanthropy.

It will be noticed that Liberia has adopted a plan for the suppression of the slave-trade. There are few subjects more deserving of the earnest and immediate attention of all the friends of mankind.

Consulate General of Liberia,
*London, May* 18, 1860.

My Lord: When I had the honor of some conversation with your lordship, a few days ago, I promised that I would give the particulars of my efforts to have the "slave-trade" denounced as piracy, in the treaties I was negotiating on behalf of the Republic of Liberia. Since my interview with your lordship, I have signed a treaty of amity, commerce and navigation with the Marquis d'Azeglio, the minister plenipotentiary of Sardinia. Having settled all the articles, I have arranged to sign a similar treaty with M. de Bille, the minister plenipotentiary of Denmark, on the 21st inst.

I was lately instructed by the President of Liberia to endeavor to get an article, denouncing slave-trade *as piracy*, inserted in all the treaties I might negotiate with foreign powers, and accordingly I proposed to both these ministers that the article should be in the following words, viz: "The slave-trade is piracy, and shall be *so* treated by the two contracting parties." These gentlemen, having referred to their respective governments at Turin and Copenhagen, declined sanctioning the phraseology proposed by me, but Sardinia offered a substitute as follows, viz: "La traite des noirs est rigouresement defendue; les navirs de deux Etats qui se livreraient a cet infame traffic, deront juges et punis d'apres les lois en vigueur dans leur pays respectiff." Denmark presented the following, viz: "The slave-trade is prohibited and declared criminal by the two contracting parties."

Both Sardinia and Denmark have the most stringent and severe laws against the slave-trade, but neither country was willing to consider it in the light of piracy; and although both these substitutes are very mild compared with my proposition, I was glad to get them rather than to obtain no denunciation of this infamous traffic, which, if proscribed and treated by all the maritime powers of the world as piracy, would be the best means of eradicating this crime against civilization and humanity.

Both the Republics—the United States of America, and Liberia—have declared slave-trade to be piracy, and I wish all the commercial nations of the earth would imitate their good example. Although the American flag is most lamentably prostituted to protect slave-trade,* I am happy to say that Liberia, ever since its existence as an independent State, has manifested the strongest hostility to this accursed trade, and has been eminently successful, by the destruction of baracoons and slave vessels, to destroy it upon its seven hundred miles of coast, where, previously to the foundation of this youthful State, this abominable traffic abounded. Now, the cultivation of sugar, coffee, cotton, &c., and the collection of palm oil, camwood, and other articles of legitimate commerce, have taken the place of the greatest of all evils—slave-trade.

Knowing the kind interest which your lordship takes in our youthful Republic, as well as in all efforts to ameliorate the unhappy condition of the African race, I hope I may be excused for writing so long a letter, and that I may be allowed to subscribe myself, with great respect and consideration, your lordship's most obedient servant,

GERARD RALSTON.

To the Right Honorable Lord Brougham.

Translation of article proposed by Sardinia

"The slave-trade is rigorously prohibited; the vessels of the two States which may be engaged in this infamous traffic shall be tried and punished according to the laws in force in their respective countries."

## The Chartered Ships for Recaptured Africans.

THE Financial Secretary has furnished us with the following brief statement of his proceedings in the charter and outfit of three large ships to convey the recaptured Africans (nearly 1,300 by last accounts) now at Key West, to their African homes in Liberia:

The ship "Castilian," of 1,025 tons, well found, and fitted out in every respect in accordance with the United States passenger law, sailed from New York the 10th of June, 1860, for Liberia, via of Key West, to carry, say about 450 of the wild Africans, mentioned in our last, and land them at Cape Mount. Instructions have been given to our

* The stars and stripes will ever be thus desecrated until America and England agree upon the mutual right of search within certain latitudes. It is unworthy of our great country to be so sensitive and to refuse to grant this reasonable proposition of "search." For a mighty empire to stand upon its dignity in 1860, and refuse the right of search, which it properly denied when a feeble nation, in 1812, shows little self-respect, little self-reliance, little consciousness of its great power. When an insignificant State, as she was in 1812, and resented the compulsory search by the English frigate Leopard of the United States frigate Constellation, in the Chesapeake Bay, was right enough, and showed "pluck," which I hope all Anglo-Saxons will manifest on proper occasions; but to refuse this right of search (under proper restrictions) *now*, when the American flag is as much esteemed for its protecting power as that of France or Great Britain, indicates a humble—provincial—anything but a proper national feeling—little creditable to the pride with which we Americans should always uphold our country's reputation. As England is willing to grant the reciprocal right of search, why does not America free herself from this foul blot? Have my countrymen not enough love and respect for our flag to resolve that it shall no longer be polluted by protecting such nefarious traffic? G. RALSTON.

agent there to place them together on fine farming land, at some distance from the coast, in houses built for them, and to be under the care and management of superintendants and teachers, who would require them to attend school half the day and labor the other half, and at all times to conduct themselves in a manner becoming the habits of civilized life.

The ship "South Shore," of 941 tons, fitted as above, sailed the 13th June, 1860, to carry about the same number (450) to Monrovia and Bassa, to be located as far up the St. John's river as possible, in a company, to be cared for and managed as above.

The ship "Star of the Union," of 1,057 tons, chartered and fitted as above, sailed the 23d June, 1860, to take about the same number (450) to Sinou, to be located up the Sinou river as near to the falls as possible, and provided for as above.

The charter of these three ships cost $36,500 00. The expenses of their outfit of provisions and water for the passage, and for the Africans after their arrival in Liberia, have already amounted to $60,778 98.

The United States Government sent an agent in each ship to look after the comfort and general welfare of the Africans. We sent a physician in each ship, and also a cook, steward, and nurse.

We may, therefore, congratulate ourselves that every thing has been done thus far for the health and prosperity of these people.

[From the N. Y. Colonization Journal.]

## The Presbyterian Church and Colonization.

THE American Colonization Society is indebted for its origin and continued support to the Presbyterian Church pre-eminently. At Princeton, New Jersey, a company of Presbyterian ministers held a meeting in the fall of 1816 to consult upon some movement for the benefit of the free colored population, and to pray for Divine guidance and blessing. Finley and Alexander were active members of that praying circle.

In December, 1816, another meeting for prayer and consultation was held in Dr. Lauri's Presbyterian church in Washington city, at which were Lauri, Finley, Mills, and Caldwell, among others of different churches, uniting to form the new organization. These men all felt that they were serving God and promoting his glory, and spreading his kingdom, while thus engaged. At the next meeting of the General Assembly of the Presbyterian Church, held in Philadelphia, May, 1817, the objects and claims of the Society were brought before that venerable body, and cordially endorsed and recommended to the churches. A year afterward the whole question of the churches' views of slavery, and its relation to the colored race, was considered, and a memorable utterance made, in the course of which Colonization was again fully endorsed and recommended to the churches as worthy of aid.

In 1819, and often afterward, down to 1853, the General Assembly renewed their testimony, and urged the churches to give it annual collections. Here the matter rested until, at the meeting of the Assembly at Indianapolis, May, 1859, for the first time in forty-two years there was an apparent change of policy.

On Monday, May 30th, Dr. R. R.

Reed, an elder from the church at Washington, Pennsylvania, offered resolutions reaffirming the confidence of the Assembly in the Colonization Society, and commending its object.

After some discussion, they were referred to the committee on bills and overtures.

At the evening session, Tuesday, May 31st, Dr. Rice, from the committee on bills and overtures, made a favorable report of these resolutions, and his report was accepted and placed on the docket.

The press of business was so great that this report was not reached on the docket until Thursday morning, June 2d, when scarcely a quorum was present, and all were anxious for an adjournment. When it was taken up, Dr. Thornwell, of South Carolina, took ground against any action, on the general ground that it was not competent for the General Assembly to take cognizance of any society, however excellent, outside of its own control—an argument as applicable to the Bible Society as to the Colonization Society. Wearied out by an apparent intention to make delay, and anxious to leave, the whole subject was laid on the table.

This was an event alike surprising and painful to the many Christian hearts, which, under the guidance of previous Assemblies, had learned to love, and pray, and labor for this Society as a noble instrument by which mercy and justice could in some manner reach poor Africa. It is not wonderful, therefore, that the course which might be taken by the Assembly at its recent meeting in Rochester was looked forward to with very great interest.

We attended the sessions of the Assembly, arriving there on the 23d of May, and the fifth day of the session. We found the subject had come up on an overture from the Synod of Wheeling, and was there before the committee of bills and overtures. Dr. Scott, of San Francisco, formerly of New Orleans, was chairman of the committee.

The committee made no report until the 30th of May, when, instead of the former clear, open, noble endorsement of the Colonization Society on its own merits, it was vaguely referred to as follows:

In relation to the several memorials and overtures referred to the committee relating to Colonization, Temperance, the Slave Trade, etc., the committee recommended the adoption of the following resolution, viz.:

*Resolved*, That while the General Assembly on the one hand disclaim all right to interfere in secular matters, and on the other assert the right and duty of the church, as God's witness on earth, to bear her testimony in favor of truth and holiness, and against all false doctrines and views, wherever professed and committed, yet, in view of the often repeated action of the Assembly in reference to the subjects above referred to, it is inexpedient to take any further action in relation thereto.

This was unanimously adopted, without debate.

In relation to the above resolution, we especially call attention to the reference made to "*the often repeated action of the Assembly in reference to these subjects*."

We see no other possible explanation of this language than that by unanimous consent this Assembly adopts the action of all former sessions, and abides by them, as sufficiently declaring its present views.

We, therefore, that our readers may know just what this "repeated action of the Assembly" has been, reproduce it, as found ready at our hands in Dr. Baird's Compendium.

Resolutions in favor of Colonization, and recommendations of it to the churches as worthy of aid by annual collections, by "repeated action" from 1817 to 1853, and now referred to in 1860 by the late Assembly are so clear and satisfactory that it is inexpedient to take action in relation thereto.

AMERICAN COLONIZATION SOCIETY.

§ 48.

[The American Colonization Society was organized Dec. 21, 1816. In May, 1817.]

"The Assembly notice with pleasure the general attention and exertion to alleviate the condition of the people of color in almost all parts of the country. A Society for the Colonization of free people of this description is formed, and is patronized by the first characters of our nation."—*Minutes*, 1817, p. 651.

§ 49.

"Having thus expressed our views of slavery, and of the duty indispensably incumbent on all Christians to labor for its complete extinction, we proceed to recommend, and we do it with all the earnestness and solemnity which this momentous subject demands, a particular attention to the following points:

*(e)* "We recommend to all our people to patronize and encourage the Society lately formed for colonizing in Africa, the land of their ancestors, the free people of color in our country. We hope that much good may result from the plans and efforts of this Society. And while we exceedingly rejoice to have witnessed its origin and organization among the holders of slaves, as giving an unequivocal pledge of their desires to deliver themselves and their country from the calamity of slavery; we hope that those portions of the American Union whose inhabitants are by a gracious Providence more favorably circumstanced will cordially, and liberally, and earnestly co-operate with their brethren in bringing about the great end contemplated."—*Minutes*, 1818.

§ 50.

"The following overture was submitted to the Assembly, which, being read and amended, was adopted, viz:

"The objects and plans of the American Society for Colonizing the free people of color of the United States, having been stated to the General Assembly, and the same having been considered and discussed, the Assembly

"*Resolved*, That, in their opinion, the plan of the Society is benevolent in its design, and if properly supported, and judiciously and vigorously prosecuted, calculated to be extensively useful to this country and to Africa.

"The situation of the people of color in this country has frequently attracted the attention of this Assembly. In the distinctive and indelible marks of their color, and the prejudices of the people, an insuperable obstacle has been placed to the execution of any plan for elevating their character, and placing them on a footing with their brethren of the same common family. In restoring them to the land of their fathers, the Assembly hope that the way may be opened, not only for the accomplishment of that object, but for introducing civilization and the Gospel to the benighted nations of Africa.

"From the information and statements received, the Assembly believe that the proposed colony in Africa may be made a powerful auxiliary to the efforts which are making to abolish the iniquitous traffic in slaves carried on in Africa, and happily calculated to lay the foundation of a gradual emancipation of slaves in our own country, in a legal and constitutional manner, and without violating the rights or injuring the feelings of our Southern brethren.

"With these views, the Assembly feel it a duty to recommend the American Society for Colonizing the free people of color of the United States, to the patronage and attention of the churches under their care, and to benevolent individuals throughout the Union."—*Minutes*, 1819, *p.* 710.

§ 51. FOURTH OF JULY COLLECTIONS RECOMMENDED.

"*Resolved,* That this Assembly recommend to the churches under their care to patronize the objects of the American Colonization Society, and particularly that they take up collections in aid of its funds on the 4th of July next, or on the Sabbath immediately preceding or succeeding that day, and whenever such course may be thought expedient, to give their assistance in such manner as may be most conducive to the interests of the general cause."—*Minutes*, 1825.

[This recommendation has been again and again reiterated. See *Minutes*, 1816, p. 26; 1828, p. 238; 1831, p. 184; 1832, p. 326; 1833, p. 497; 1839, p. 155.]

§ 52.

(*a*) "1. *Resolved,* That the enterprise of the Colonization Society, so successfully prosecuted amid so much obloquy, opposition, and misunderstanding, has our highest confidence, as wise, peaceful, humane, and philanthropic.

"*Resolved,* That as it has been in past years repeatedly commended to the patronage of the churches in our connection as pre-eminently combining the noblest benefits to Africa and America, to the emigrant colonists, and to the heathen tribes around them, we would again offer it to their patronage, and most earnestly recommend to all pastors and churches an annual collection for its support, to be made early in July.

"3. *Resolved,* That we have heard with the highest pleasure of the complete destruction of the slave factories near Liberia, and most earnestly hope for the day when a traffic so odious and cruel shall be swept from the ocean."—*Minutes*, 1848, p. 32.

(*b*) "*Resolved,* That the cause of Colonization be recommended to the favor and support of the churches."—*Minutes*, 1853, p. 459.

[From the Colonization Herald.]

## Encouraging Progress.

THE colony of Sierra Leone, and the Republic of Liberia, on the Western Coast of Africa, are noble monuments of England's and America's philanthropic exertions. They were established and are sustained on the true and only principles of Christian colonization. And they are fulfilling the hopes of their founders and supporters, in standing forth as centres of light to the surrounding darkness. The population of Sierra Leone is computed to exceed sixty thousand souls, and is composed of members of some sixty tribes of Africans, speaking as many different dialects. They were mostly rescued by British cruisers from slavers, carried to this asylum, and afforded the advantages of education and civilization. Hundreds of them are now well qualified ministers of the gospel, catechists, teachers, and merchants. Several of the latter named class have acquired more than one hundred thousand dollars; others own vessels of considerable size, and navigate them themselves Many have sent their children to Europe for education and a knowledge of mechanic arts

Liberia is the vigorous off-spring of the benevolence of the United States. It affords an inviting home to the people of color of this country, extirpates slavery and the slave trade from its territory, is establishing an honorable nationality for the race, and has laid a foundation where Christianity is rearing her temples and civilization, her halls of science and literature.. [It has many ministers, churches, and communicants, and one hundred teachers.] Nearly twelve thousand American colored persons have been settled in Liberia by the Colonization Society, and these, with over two hundred thousand natives, have become an independent nation, with a republican constitution, securing to its citizens all the privileges of civil freedom. The industry of the aborigines is encouraged, and the resources of the land are being developed. A large, profitable, and increasing export trade is carried on. In addition to a considerable number of small craft engaged in the coasting trade, several Liberian houses run vessels to New York and Baltimore. The Eusebia N. Roye is the name of a brig which, with her cargo, is owned by Mr. Roye, a black merchant of Monrovia, who sails her with Liberian papers and the Liberian flag.

The several armed squadrons, organized and enlightened governments, legitimate commerce, and zealous missionaries, are doing much for Western Africa. Indeed, the amount of good already secured in this portion of the great continent very far exceeds the most sanguine anticipations. Bishop Payne, of the Episcopal Mission at Cape Palmas, and who has labored in this part of the Continent for twenty-two years, recently stated that there was scarcely a village between the Gambia and the mouth of the Gaboon, a distance of two thousand miles, where a traveller would not be at least saluted by a native in the English tongue. Along this whole extent where, forty years ago, all was barren and unchristian, the language has been written in twenty-five dialects. There are one hundred church buildings, two hundred schools, and over sixteen thousand children, while the Gospel is preached to over five millions of Africans. Truly, there is hope for Africa, and for the elevation of the colored race. May all concerned realize and act up to their responsibilities.

## Increase of Emigration, and Annual Collections.

WHAT shall be done? The free colored population, aroused by the developments of the past year better to appreciate the advantages presented by Africa, and the difficulties in their path here, are, in numbers far beyond any previous time, applying for aid to emigrate. Shall the aid they seek be granted by the Society? Will the philanthropic and Christian community furnish the needful means? The calls for Bibles, and tracts, and missionaries, for the foreign and home work, are taxing the churches for increased contributions almost beyond their ability. But can we afford to stop the Colonization work? Can we say to these people, Yes, we have all along said you had better go and form a Christian nation in Africa—we have invited you to go, and offered aid; but now that you are willing, we must refuse to give it?

Surely every motive which ever justified the Colonization work still exists with increasing force. The condition of the colored freeman here is not more promising; the benefits to Africa are not less real; the need of an asylum for the poor slave, emancipated from the slave ship by our cruisers, or set free by the self-denying benevolence of masters, is not less urgent.

Indeed, by the rapid capture of slaver after slaver, lately made, we are compelled with new earnestness to wish that Liberia had fifty thousand emigrants from our country, instead of the handful now there.

We ask all who have, as individuals, or as organized churches, hitherto extended aid to the Society, to renew their benefactions again this year. Never has our claim been stronger, or our need greater.—*N. Y. Col. Journal.*

## Fourth of July Contributions.

No occasion can be esteemed more proper, for all who desire the success of African Colonization, to make contributions to its aid, than on that day, so signal in the annals of our beloved country, and the celebration of which is so near at hand.

To unite with the rites of our national jubilee, yearly advances for the infant African Republic; to bear in recollection the struggle now making to restore to the land of their forefathers an oppressed population; to civilize and Christianize a new continent, and to effectually extirpate the inhuman and illegal slave trade, must add beyond estimation to the feeling of devotion which every American citizen now entertains for that sacred day which made him a freeman.

Influenced by these considerations, the Pennsylvania Colonization Society most earnestly entreat the clergymen of all denominations, upon the approaching anniversary of American Independence, or the Sabbath immediately preceding or succeeding the same, to call upon all who feel an interest in the success of our enterprise, to assist its progress, by all reasonable contributions.—*Colonization Herald.*

## Recaptured Africans.

President Buchanan has, by placing steamers on the African and West India stations, deserved, as he has, the cordial thanks of all who detest this murderous piracy of slave-stealing. The increased efficiency of steamers in the detection of these miscreants, is clearly demonstrated by the late captures on the east end and southern shore of Cuba.

His recommendation to Congress for a liberal appropriation for their return to Africa, and support of them, is no less praiseworthy, despite the opposition of the Garrisonians on the one side, and the Lamars and their sympathizers on the other.

We rejoice that a ready response was made by Congress to the President's message, and the sum of $250,000 placed at his disposal for this purpose. We learn that the efficient Financial Secretary of the

American Colonization Society has been several days in New York chartering vessels and purchasing needful supplies of provisions, clothing, etc., and that with all possible promptness the survivors will be conveyed to Liberia. We say survivors, for already accounts are received of dreadful mortality among these poor victims of avarice and cruelty; and if we may judge of them by the case of those captured in the Echo, not one-half embarked in Africa will live to reach there again. Why cannot some adequate punishment be inflicted on these wholesale murderers? How can any portion of our Christian land be blinded so as not to see and denounce these enormities? The only ray of comfort to be found, as we look at their hard lot, is in the existence of such an asylum in Liberia as has been prepared by the wise forethought and Christian philanthropy of America. There we may hope that they will be instructed and Christianized, by the activity of missionary societies, amid the peace and quiet of a free Christian Republic.—*N. Y. Col. Journal.*

## Christianizing Africa.

AT the present moment, owing to various causes, the eyes of many persons are turned to different schemes for christianizing Africa. Sierra Leone was the first of the modern colonies that were commenced, with the view of effecting this, and there are now about four hundred thousand nominal Christians in that colony, or under the influence of the missions of Great Britain along the coast. It was first settled as a place of refuge for those negroes who had joined the English in the revolutionary war. Nova Scotia was found too cold for them. So it was proposed to Christianize them, and form them into a missionary colony for the enlightenment of Africa. The influence has been great and good on the surrounding country, forming a great depot for the restoration of those captured by the British cruisers in efforts to suppress the slave-trade.

Liberia has proved in every respect much more successful. It is healthy and enterprising, and may be considered one of the most hopeful colonies now in existence. There is no reason why it should not in the next two hundred years do as much for the civilization and spread of Christianity in Africa, as the small colonies planted on Plymouth Rock and at Jamestown have done for the North American continent.

At this moment there are perhaps five millions of nominal Christians on the African continent, three millions of whom are Monophysites or members of the Greek Church, one million are Roman Catholics, and another million Protestants. There are one hundred millions of Mohamedans, and the rest, untold and unknown as to numbers, are heathens.—*Public Ledger.*

[From the N. H. Statesman.]

## New Hampshire Colonization Society.

THE annual meeting of the New Hampshire Colonization Society was held on the evening of the 14th instant, in the First Baptist (Rev. Dr. Flanders') church, in this city (Concord.)

Although several public gatherings occurred on that evening, the spacious church was filled with a large and appreciative audience. The President of the Society, Rev. Dr. Burroughs, of Portsmouth, occupied the chair. The meeting was opened with prayer by Rev. Dr. Flanders.

The meeting was favored with an address from the President, of great beauty and force, and enlisted the close attention of the assembly. He seemed thoroughly imbued with the spirit of colonization; he sketched, as with a master's hand, the picture of Africa's ancient grandeur and renown; how learning, civilization, and the arts passed from Egypt to Etruria, from Etruria to Rome, from Rome to England, and from England to America, leaving their original abode, enveloped in barbarism and darkness. But through the agency of colonization, the speaker believed a brighter day was soon to dawn on that unfortunate land; and her future, when civilization and commerce should have developed her vast resources, was drawn in glowing colors, and made a deep impression.

The meeting was then addressed by Rev. John Orcutt, Travelling Secretary of the American Colonization Society. The claims of this Society always find an able advocate in Mr. Orcutt; and on the present occasion the great growing interest in the colonization of Africa with free people of color, was dwelt upon with great effect.

The friends of the cause were gratified by the presence of His Excellency GOVERNOR GOODWIN, who appeared on the platform with other distinguished gentlemen.—Upon the conclusion of Mr. Orcutt's remarks, His Excellency addressed to the meeting a few very earnest and highly interesting remarks, expressive of his deep sense of the importance of the cause, and urging the necessity for more earnest effort in its behalf.

Upon the conclusion of Governor Goodwin's remarks, the Hon. N. G. Upham offered the following series of resolutions:

*Resolved*, That the establishment of an educated and Christianized Colony of the Colored Race on the Continent of Africa, with the full powers of a sovereign and independent State, furnishes an opportunity greatly to be desired to do away with unfounded prejudices against them as a people, and we believe it is destined to be eminently successful to this end.

*Resolved*, That the Colony of Liberia has been the means of extinguishing the Slave Trade along a coast of some five hundred miles in extent, which was formerly the favorite and chief resort of slavers, and that the system of Colonization thus commenced is the most certain and effectual means of the entire overthrow of the African Slave Trade.

*Resolved*, That Colonization furnishes the most ready means of extending the benefits of civilization, commerce, and the arts in Africa, and with them the light and benefit of the Christian religion, and that longer delay on the part of the Christian public to aid in this great means of the regeneration of Africa manifests, as we believe, an evident disregard of the indications of Providence, and the requirements of Christian duty.

*Resolved*, That the Republic of Liberia furnishes the only desirable place now open to us for the return of the colored race wrongfully seized by violence in Africa and sold to slavers, and who are, from time to time, captured on the high seas, and that the condition of these unfortunate captives calls, in a high degree, for the sympathy and humanity of the American people.

*Resolved,* That the establishment of commerce, industry, and the increase of the indigenous products of Africa, will have a marked effect in making that country the true and desirable home of the colored race, and a residence there the chief object of their ambition.

The Rev. F. Butler then presented the following, which was also unanimously adopted:

*Resolved,* That the present auspicious condition of Liberia should inspire our gratitude to God.

The public services were then concluded with prayer by Rev. H. E. Parker.

The Society made choice of the following officers for the ensuing year.

Rev. CHARLES BURROUGHS, D. D., *President.*

*Vice Presidents*—Hon. N. G. Upham, Rev. Prof. D. J. Noyes, D. D., Hon. William Haile, Rev. John K. Young, D D., Hon. Joel Eastman, Rev. Z. S. Barstow, D. D., Simeon Ide, Esq., Hon. John H. White, Hon. Isaac Spalding.

*Secretary*—Samuel G. Lane, Esq.

*Treasurer*—J. C. A. Wingate, Esq.

*Managers*—J. B. Walker, Esq. Rev. Prof. Patten, Rev. C. W. Flanders, D. D., Rev. H. E. Parker, Horace Webster, Esq., Onslow Stearns, Esq., L. T. Flint, Esq.

A vote was passed that every clergyman in the State should be requested to present the subject of Colonization to his people once in each year.

The interest in this cause is evidently on the increase, and it is to be hoped that it will at no distant day assume the position which it deserves among the great philanthropic enterprises of the day.

[From the Presbyterian.]

## The Ashmun Institute.

THE Ashmun Institute is chartered by the Legislature of Pennsylvania, with the privileges of a college. It is open to all colored men who submit to its regulations and laws. It is located near Oxford, in Chester County, Pennsylvania, and will be accessible from the Elk Dale Station, on the New Philadelphia and Baltimore Central Railroad. It derives its name from Jehudi Ashmun, the founder of the Colony of Liberia, and is given out of respect to his memory. It was established by, and is under the direction of the Presbytery of New Castle, a Presbytery of the Old School Presbyterian Church, having 9 Trustees, chosen by that Presbytery, to serve three years each, or until others are appointed in their place.

The more direct and special object in view is to provide a competent ministry for the colored population of this country, and to prepare missionaries and teachers for Africa. From the most reliable data it appears there are about sixteen thousand colored persons within the bounds of the Newcastle Presbytery; and there are forty congregations of this class of persons regularly meeting for religious worship within the same bounds, without one properly qualified minister to preach the gospel to them. This is, in a measure, their condition in all parts of our country, while we know of no academy or college under proper influence where they can be admitted on equal terms with others, to receive a thorough education.

The Institute holds thirty acres of land, beautifully located, in which are a college building, capable of accommodating thirty or more students, and a President's house; these buildings are of brick, and very substantial. Classes have been regularly instructed since January, 1857, and there are now twelve young men of promise connected with them; two of these have been sent for the purpose from Liberia; five at least are preparing for the ministry, and among the number are members of the Episcopal, Old and New School Presbyterian, and Baptist Churches. The tuition is offered gratuitously, with room and furniture, and most of the pupils are indebted to benevolent individuals and churches, as well as to the Education Boards of the several denominations, for the means of meeting other expenses. The Institution presents to the Christian and the philanthropist an opportunity of doing good to the colored race, and without interfering with their civil or social condition; its ecclesiastical connection affords a guarantee that it will be conducted so as not to give offence to any reasonable person. Contributions are earnestly solicited to sustain the Trustees in carrying out the object of the Institution. There is no paid agency for collecting funds, and we trust that, by God's blessing, they will be offered voluntarily, as they have been in a measure.

Three missionaries, the first graduates of the Institution, have been sent to Africa the present year, to establish a new mission, under the care of the Foreign Presbyterian Board.

The Session commences on the 1st of August, and continues for ten months. Ten dollars per month pays all the expenses of the Institution for each pupil.

*President of the Faculty.*

Rev. John P. Carter.

*Board of Trustees.*

Rev. Joseph McElroy, D. D., of the Presbytery of New York; Rev. William Chester, D. D., of the Presbytery of Philadelphia; Rev. James Latta, of the Presbytery of Newcastle; Rev. J. B. Spotswood, D. D., of the Presbytery of Newcastle; Rev. Alfred Hamilton, D. D., of the Presbytery of Chicago; Rev. John M. Dickey, D. D., of the Presbytery of Newcastle.

*Ruling Elders.*

John M. Kelton, Esq., Samuel J. Dickey, Esq., William Wilson, Esq.

The Presbytery of Newcastle, on the 5th of October, 1853, adopted the following:

"Considering the many Christian congregations of colored people in this country which are unable to secure educated ministers of their own color; considering the communities of such people in many parts who need educated men amongst them to fill the place of teachers and other responsible situations; considering the wants of Liberia, and importance to its present and future welfare of having suitably qualified men to fill its offices and posts of authority, instruction and influence; considering the vast missionary work yet to be done in Africa, and to be done mainly by colored men; considering how extremely difficult it is for colored youth to obtain a liberal education in this land, arising from the want of schools for that purpose, and their exclusion from the most of the regular institutions of learning of higher grade; considering the strong recommendation to that effect from our Board of Education, and its full endorsement by the General Assembly of our Church; and considering the favorable indications of Providence at this time apparently calling us to such a work, this Presbytery, trusting in God, and, under him, depending on the Christian liberality of the friends of the African race throughout our country, do determine that there shall be established within our bounds, and under our supervision, an institution to be called the Ashmun Institute, for the scientific, classical and theological education of colored youth of the male sex."

The General Assembly of the Presbyterian Church, at Nashville, Tennessee, in May, 1855, adopted the following:

"1. *Resolved,* That this General Assembly has heard with pleasure of the design and practical effort, on the part of the Presbytery of Newcastle, to establish a school in which colored young men of piety may receive a thorough classical and theological education, fitting them for the work of the ministry, and teaching among the destitute thousands of this country, and the millions of Africa.

"2. *Resolved,* That we regard this work as an important preliminary work aiming at the highest good of the African race wherever found; and hereby express our cordial approbation of it, and recommend our churches cheerfully and liberally to co-operate in this work of faith and labor."

We refer to the report of the Board of Education to the General Assembly in May, 1853, and also to subsequent reports, as containing very earnest recommendations of the Ashmun Institute.

JOHN M. DICKEY,
*Chairman Ex. Com.*

☞Contributions may be sent either to Wm. Rankin, Esq., Treasurer of the Board of Foreign Missions, No. 23 Centre Street, New York; William Main, Esq., Treasurer of the Board of Education, No. 821 Chestnut street, Philadelphia, or to the Chairman of the Executive Committee named above.

## Missionary Intelligence.

### YORUBA, AFRICA.

The Baptist Southern Board of Missions has suffered some severe reverses in the return of missionaries. Brother Priest and his family have come to the United States. Brother Phillips regards the prospect of the Mission as hopeful. He says:

"My connection with the Board has now been more than five years, and on my part the connection has been a very pleasant one. * * * We are all getting on very well here. I hope we grow in favor with the people every day. You know how much we need laborers here, so I need not urge you to send us any.

* * * *

I am looking with interest to several who attend our services on Sabbath and give some signs of interest. I have had very interesting conversations with Mahommedans, of late. I seldom preach through an interpreter."

### AWYAW.

Our lone missionary, T. A. Reed, is here. His health is feeble, but he is not discouraged. He is laboring in the dispensation of the gospel with great fidelity, and looks forward to large success, if the proper means are pursued. The pressing necessity of reinforcements is urged by him, and he expresses the desirableness of securing colored men to aid in the work. He remarks, that we need a strong reinforcement none will doubt or deny; yet we hear of no one buckling on the armor of the gospel and heeding the Macedonian cry, "Come over and help us." Brethren, is this right in the sight of God? Are you content to lave your brows in the waters of forgetfulness till every missionary impression is forever extinguished? * * * *

LIBERIA.

In connection with this Mission, we have found reason for lamentation, and for increased thankfulness and joy. * * * The Board were deeply affected by the removal of such men as Day and Cheeseman, and felt anxiously concerned in reference to the increase of suitable men for this field. We have been favored with finding brother J. J. Fitzgerald, who has entered upon his labors, and brother George W. Parker, who is expected soon to depart for this field.

SIERRA LEONE.

This mission is connected with that in Liberia, and under the same general management. There are two stations, Freetown and Waterloo. The former of these is occupied by brother J. J. Brown, the latter by brother George S. Weeks There is a school at each station.

---

MRS. MILES, a missionary of the American Missionary Society, died on the 16th of March, at the Boon Falls Station, in the Mendi Country. She sailed for Africa with her husband November 17, 1855. She died with affecting expressions on her lips of love to the African children she had taught, and with prayer that she might be taken to her Lord.

"'And is this death?' 'Yes,' I said; 'you don't mind it, do you?' '*Calm*,' she answered. 'I have been happy all the time since I have been here in Africa. Oh, that I might live for these children.' To me she said: '*Do all you can for Africa, and meet me in heaven.*'"

The American Missionary adds:

After bidding farewell to those around her, and some expressions of fond endearments to her husband, she raised her finger, pointing upward, and said: "O Jesus, come quickly; come soon." Her prayer was soon answered; she drew a few short breaths, and passed away.

"Thus," says one who knew her well, "with no regret that she had gone to Africa, with an unshaken trust in her Redeemer, she died as any Christian might wish to die. Her constitution had been frail many years, and it was of course a doubtful problem how the African climate would affect it. She longed to go. She went, and is probably the sooner in heaven; and probably, too, was the sooner ripe for those mansions The testimony borne to the Gospel spirit, by such a life and such a death, may be worth more than many lives. There can be no greater mistake than to account such a life and death a failure."

---

[From the Missionary Advocate.]

BISHOP BURNS writes in relation to the native youth in the families of our missionaries, to be educated on what is called Bishop Scott's plan: "If you could have but witnessed the death of one of these native boys, who had learned to know the power of Jesus' name, it would have more than compensated you for all the expense you have been put to in educating these youths."

EXPLORING THE INTERIOR.—There is quite a tendency among the intelligent members of the Republic of Liberia to visit the interior to ascertain the resources of the country.

The agreement of the visitors in the reports which they make of the inviting appearance for the presence of Christian missionaries and those in pursuit of an extended commerce with the natives, is very striking.

Rev. J. Seys, whose interest in the colonization scheme is well known, writes:

"My own opinion is that Liberia has at present territory enough coast wise. To the interior, the elevated, undulating, healthy mountains and valleys of the interior, let her send her coming and increasing population. Let Carysburg, with its rapid improvements and natural resources, be but the beginning of a number of such settlements. Let New Jersey persevere in her settlement of Bassa. Let Pennsylvania furnish us with twenty families, and means to locate them on the Junk river, that fine, healthy, rich country, where millions of acres of land invite the immigrant to come and be rich and happy."

Education for Africa.—The Ashmun Institute, located at Oxford, Chester county, Pennsylvania, was chartered by the Legislature of that State, and is now open as a college and theological seminary for colored men. The school has been in operation for over three years, and several of its graduates are now laboring in Western Africa, in the capacity of missionaries of the Presbyterian church. Twelve pupils are at present prosecuting their studies under its control and direction, two of whom are from Liberia.

The Republic of Liberia.—Our commercial interests with this young nation greatly need the serious attention of Congress, however they may regard other interests in connection with that republic. We think the following extract will interest alike the friends of American missions and of American commerce in Africa:

"The commerce of Western Africa is estimated at from twenty to fifty millions of dollars annually. Hundreds of vessels sail along its coast from almost every nation. The great majority of them, however, belong to British merchants. What is the proportion of American interest in this trade, and what is our government doing to open it up to our people, and to foster it and protect them in its prosecution? President Fillmore sent a large naval fleet, with costly presents, to Japan, to invite the commerce of that distant nation. A powerful squadron watches over and guards our intercourse with far-off China. But here is a continent close to our own, with an already valuable traffic, whose resources are only beginning to be known, and 'whose wants are capable of doubling even the clatter of every loom, and the ring of every anvil in Europe and America.' What are our rulers doing to secure for the country an interest in the Liberian-African trade? Not only absolutely nothing, but by the operation of existing laws is it being driven away from our shores to be monopolized by England, whose policy attracts, and hence is securing it. The following facts will prove this, and likewise show how we discriminate against ourselves:

"Last summer the brig *Eusebia N. Roye* arrived at New York from Liberia, being the first vessel that ever brought the Liberian flag to the United States. Her load of African produce yielded over twenty thousand dollars. Her owner, Mr. Edward J. Roye, is a black man, who emigrated from Ohio in 1840, and has since resided at Monrovia, where he has been successfully engaged in mercantile affairs. Mr. Roye was compelled to pay some two hundred dollars as tonnage duty, in addition to the duty upon the goods, because our government has not yet formed a formal treaty with Liberia. The unjustness of this toward a feeble power is the more to be regretted as, by the Liberian custom, the vessels of the United States and their contents stand on the same equality as those of the most favored nations.

"Great Britain, France, Belgium, and other European powers have not only recognized the independence of Liberia, but have entered into treaties of amity and commerce with the young African republic. If, through mere squeamishness in certain quarters, our Government will not acknowledge the former, ought it to neglect or refuse the latter, when all the benefit will accrue to our people? Such a course must divert still more this trade from us to other countries. That a vessel from Liberia entering our waters should be compelled to pay about one dollar per ton more than one belonging to Turkey, Japan, or China, seems most unreasonable. Is it possible that Mohammedans and Pagans can thus trade with us on better terms than a Christian people, who have, with the approval, and, to some extent, with the co-operation of our government, founded, and are conducting a free and independent state on the shores of Africa?

"Let us hope that our statesmen will take hold of this subject, and seek to have Liberian trade and shipping put on the same footing which that power extends to ours. Deeply will Africa's productiveness affect the markets of the world. Let us get and retain an interest in the commerce of this mighty continent. Our people want the productions of Africa to come to America, and American manufactures to reach Africa. Ought not their wishes to be heeded by those in authority?"

---

Death of a Missionary.—That excellent Missionary, the Rev. C. C. Hoffman, of the Episcopal Mission, (for the last ten years at Cape Palmas,) writes from Goshen, New York, June 1, 1860:

"I had a letter recently from Rev. Mr. Crummell, who informs me of the death of one of our Missionaries, Miss Spaulding; whom, he says, passed away gently, almost unconsciously, without a struggle. She died on the 7th of April, in her first attack of fever, after a residence of four and a half months, during which time she appeared in the enjoyment of vigorous health.—As her strength was so were her labors. Her death has caused great sorrow in all the community. She was so frank, so cordial, so gracious in her manner, that every body admired and respected her; and such were the evidences of her sincerity and her ardor, that we know that we have experienced a great loss. Here is one more taken from our feeble hands, one more who has laid down her life for Africa."

---

Africa.—Our latest communications are dated Monrovia, February 15th, and Corisco, January 16th. At the latter place the missionaries were in the enjoyment of good health, and were still very much encouraged in their work. At their last communion, fifteen persons were received to membership of the church on a profession of their faith. Some opposition to this work of grace had manifested itself among the heathen members of the community, but to no great extent. The brethren have forwarded a request that another female teacher be sent out to aid in the missionary work. The Messrs. Amos had recently returned from a tour of observation to the falls of the Sinou river, which place they recommend as the site of their future mission. Mr. Miller had just returned to Monrovia from a tour to the Golah country on a like mission, and he requests the concurrence of the committee for the establishment of his mission in that part of the country.—*Presbyterian Home and Foreign Record for May.*

## Intelligence.

The Slave Trade in New York.—The New York Tribune, of June 20, states that the schooner Margaretta is strongly suspected of being fitted out for the slave trade; that information was lodged against her, but while the Japanese were landing she slipped off, and is now probably well on toward the Slave Coast. Another vessel, strongly suspected, had also taken a sudden leave of New York harbor.

"New York (says the Tribune) is fast acquiring a monopoly of this lucrative but rather hazardous traffic. We mean that it *was* hazardous; but our delegate to Charleston, who there declared himself 'with' Mr. Goulden in his willingness to re-open the slave trade, has changed all this. It is somewhat expensive to clear a slaver from this port, but it has ceased to be extra hazardous."

---

Rev. G. R. Girardeau.—The Southern Baptist speaks highly of this young colored preacher, pastor of a colored congregation in Charleston, consisting mostly of slaves, with a few colored free people:

"The church in which he preaches was built exclusively for the colored people, and they regularly fill all its pews, while only a few of the multitude of white persons who are anxious to hear him can crowd around the pulpit, or stand in the isles. Here, thrice on the Sabbath, and two or three times in the week, he delivers to twelve or fifteen hundred colored people, those eloquent and fervid discourses which distinguish him above all his brethren of the same age. The fruits of his labors for the past year have been about one hundred conversions in his own congregation, and a goodly number of his casual white hearers, who have united with other churches. As he is only 28 years of age, we trust that his usefulness as a preacher of righteousness is mainly in the future, and that the Lord may long spare him to labor in his vineyard, in the exercise of those gifts with which he has signally favored him."

---

The Last Slave Vessel Sent to Key West.—A letter from on board the U. States steamer Crusader, gives an account of the last capture of a slaver which has been reported, an unknown vessel under French colors. The loathsome odor of a crowded slave ship was distinguished at intervals as the steamer approached her, and also by the boats which boarded her, when at a considerable distance. The colors and papers were all thrown overboard when they found a capture inevitable. She is said to have had Portuguese papers.

As soon as the steamer's boats reached the barque, the slaves with a tremendous shout forced off the hatches and sprang on deck by hundreds. The writer says:

"They climbed up all along the rail; they hung on the shrouds; they clustered like swarming bees in the rigging, while rose from sea to sky the wildest acclamations of delight; they danced and leaped and waved their arms in the air, and screamed and yelled in a discordant but pathetic concert.

"There was one thing, however, even more touching than all this outcry of barbaric rejoicing. My attention was attracted to a group consisting of somewhat more than a hundred women withdrawn apart from the noisy men. Their behavior was in strong contrast with that of the others, and was characteristic of their sex. Entirely nude, but innocently unabashed, they sat or knelt in tearful and silent thankfulness Several of them held infants in their arms, and through their tears, like sunshire from behind a cloud, beamed an expression of the greatest gratitude and happiness. The men looked as though they had just been raised from despair to the most exultant gladness; but with the women it seemed as though resignation and patient suffering had been changed into hope and gentle joy.

"I could not help being reminded of Mungo Park's simple and touching account of the kindness and gentleness of the African women as contrasted with the unfeeling cruelty of the men—a fact confirmed by my own experience in different parts of Guinea and along the western coast of Africa.

"Another striking thing about these women was their submissive meekness—a trait of character well described by Michelet. He says the African woman is of gentle and childlike humility—never sure of pleasing—always ready to do anything in order to displease less. No tyranny wearies her obedience; she can only tremble and ask your pardon. Of course there are some exceptions to this rule, as in the Amazon Army of the King of Dahomey, which consists of 12,000 women trained to deeds of blood and rapine.

"The first use the slaves made of their liberty was to satisfy their hunger and thirst, which they did by breaking into the bread barrels and water casks, and then running about eating, drinking, dancing, and screaming all at once. It mattered little to them what sort of vessels they drank from; buckets, boxes, and troughs were all brought into requisition. I even saw several fellows, happy and delighted, with a piece of bread in one hand and a wooden spittoon, full of muddy water, in the other.

"As soon as their appetites were satisfied, the African fondness for finery began to show itself, and all the loose articles in the ship were employed as personal ornaments. Some fastened belaying pins to their wrists; some tied old rusty tin kettles around their waists, and some strutted proudly about, with copper ladles hung round their necks.

"By this time, however a detachment of marines arrived from the Crusader, and order was at once restored. The negroes were clothed with pieces of canvas, and the captain, supercargo, and crew sent on board the Crusader as prisoners. They stated that the barque had no name, and that all their papers had been thrown overboard with the colors. They seemed to bear their loss with philosophic equanimity. Such a contingency had evidently been regarded by them as part of their risk. and they were not unprepared for it. The captain is a Frenchman, as is also the supercargo, and the crew are mostly Spaniards, with a few Frenchmen. The negroes were selected from among three thousand prisoners of war, recently taken by the King of Dahomey. They were brought from Whydah, a large town on the slave coast, in the Bight of Benin, the seaport of the renowned kingdom of Dahomey. They are much superior to the "Congos," who usually compose the cargoes of slavers, not only in physique, but also in intelligence. Nearly all are in excellent health, which, no doubt, is owing to the careful arrangements made for their comfort on board the barque. In numbers they amount to about four hundred and fifty, and the slave-deck affords ample accommodations for them all. During a passage of forty-five days from the Gulf of Guinea seven only have died, which is certainly a very small number."—*Boston Traveller, June 7.*

HORRIBLE FATE OF A CARGO OF SLAVES.—The New York Herald has a letter from Loando, West Coast of Africa, dated February 15th, giving the following horrible details:

"The principal bit of news I have to offer this time is the loss of one of our Baltimore slavers, as fine looking a clipper built hermaphrodite brig as ever was seen about these waters On the 10th of this month, as her Majesty's steamer Gloucester was cruising to the southward of Cape Lopez, they made a sail to leeward. They immediately put her before the wind to give chase, which manœuvre the fellow observing, he immediately followed suit, with a view of rounding Cape Lopez, and probably escaping after nightfall, by running into some of the small rivers inside of the Bight of Biafra. He proved himself a match, however, for his vessel sailed like a witch and gained on the steamer nearly the whole day, when, at about 5 o'clock in the afternoon, the Portuguese steamer Tagus hove in sight on the weather bow, thus cutting off the fellow's chance of rounding the cape. Seeing his chance thus lost, he stood her directly on to the rocks of the cape.

"Just before sundown the Portuguese gave him the contents of several thirty-two pounders, which brought his foretopmast down, and, as it was blowing almost a gale of wind, his jibboom followed directly after. However, the fellow stopped for nothing, and, just as night set in, drove her high on the rocks off Cape Lopez, the Portuguese steamer by that time being in close range, but the Gloucester was far behind. Those on board the other steamer, however, describe the scene as truly heartrending. As the brig struck, and was overwhelmed by the breakers, the poor miserable creatures on board, probably to the number of five hundred, set up a howl of despair that could be heard even above the roaring of the hungry sea. But it was too dark, by that time, to see much, and beyond human skill or power to aid the drowning wretches, so that they soon must have met their doom, for on the next morning the beach inside of the rocks was strewn with corpses and the fragments of the wreck. Nothing was found, however, to reveal the name of the slaver, or any other information concerning him, save that to the practised seaman she proved of Baltimore build The monsters who manned the vessel are supposed to have escaped in their boat before she struck, and must have gained the shore, as a boat somewhat stove was discovered on the beach with the oars near by. A good prize was thus lost, and, what is worse, probably five hundred human beings were launched into eternity."

THE BLIND NEGRO BOY PIANIST—HIS REMARKABLE POWERS—SINGULAR EFFECT OF HIS MUSIC UPON HIMSELF.—We have before alluded to the remarkable musical talent of the blind slave boy Tom, the property of a slaveholder in Savannah. The report of this boy's wonderful powers is thus confirmed by the Charleston Courier of January 24. The editor says:

He strikes the keys with all the confidence of one largely gifted with the musical faculty, who had devoted many years to the cultivation of the talent. His manipulation is most graceful, his touch is now exquisitely delicate, and then all the strength of his frail body is thrown into his hands, and he strikes the instrument with impassioned earnestness.

In his execution he not only reproduces the piece with perfect fidelity, giving every note its sound, but the style of the performer is likewise exactly imitated. Several of our most distinguished musicians performed in Tom's hearing long and complex operatic pieces, and the Heaven-taught boy reproduced them without committing a single mistake.

We might conclude that this boy's talent consisted in a remarkable developement of the faculties of memory and imitation, did he confine himself to those compositions he learns by the ear But he not only astonishes by the quickness with which he acquires a piece, no matter how long and difficult, but he improvises with readiness and fluency. On the occasion of which we speak, Tom was directed by his master to play an original piece, and he complied with cheerful readiness. He composed with all the ease and confidence that mark the fluent orator in the use of language.

These original compositions increase the wondering interest excited by the performance of this prodigy, and force us to look upon him as one possessed of that rare and strange gift termed genius.

We have alluded to the exquisitely

graceful touch of this lad, but what we have said concerning his manipulation gives no idea of his style and manner. For he has a style of his own, which is seen when improvising, and it is as brilliant as it is original and peculiar. But it is his manner and countenance that most profoundly impress. When not under the influence of sweet sounds, his face is devoid of life and expression. This is partly owing to blindness, but in far greater measure to imbecility. We see a boy with a decidedly African type of face—low, retreating forehead, that spreading nose and projecting upper lip, with every mark of idiotcy—we see this awkward and stupid negro led to the piano stool. He takes his seat, but the first touch on the responsive keys shows us that his soul is made for melody.

He sweeps his hands over the keys with the air of a master, and then we behold the inspiration manifesting itself in his countenance and movements till interest changes to awe, and we are dumb with astonishment. The melody penetrates his whole being. An ecstatic influence flows from the keys into his fingers, and rolls like a tide through his veins, lighting up a fire in every nerve as it courses along. His head is thrown back; now it rests on one shoulder, then on the other, and again it falls upon his breast. A light kindles on the blank face, and as we gaze, wondering, the fashion of his countenance seems changed. It is absolutely beautiful. The divine ravishment increases every moment, and when he is thoroughly diffused with the inspiration of the melody, the muscles of his face twitch, and his upper teeth are pressed firmly upon his lower lip. A feeling of reverence steals over us as we behold this mysterious and sudden transformation.

---

FERNANDO J. MORINO, the Marshal of the Southern District of Florida, writes from Key West, June 25th, "that the mortality among the recaptured Africans at that place has been great, and that he fears it has not ceased. The whole number of deaths up to this date is 222, leaving in the depot 1,209 Africans to be taken care of.

## The Colonization Society and the Government.

THE RECAPTURED AFRICANS.—It is the American Colonization Society, and not the New York State Colonization Society, as stated on Monday on the authority of a New York paper, which, under a contract with the Government, has chartered three large ships to convey the recaptured Africans from Key West to Liberia.

By last advices the number was 1,350, though some have probably since died. The superintendency of the outfit of these ships has devolved on the Rev. William McLain, Financial Secretary of the Society, whose experience and ability give assurance that the work has been well accomplished. The quiet vigor, rapidity and facility with which it was done, were remarkable.

Lest there may be some misapprehension in regard to the Colonization Society and these Africans, we are desired to say that all provision for their health and welfare is made by the Society during the voyage and for one year thereafter; that such provision includes not only all medical care, (an agent of the Government and physician and surgeon of the Society going out with them in each ship,) but accommodations, provisions, clothing, and medical stores, and medical attendance, superintendence in health as well as in sickness, and such instruction in the English language, agriculture, and the most necessary and useful arts as may suit their condition. An agent of the United States, the Rev. J. Seys, resides at Monrovia, to see to the welfare of these people, and that the benevolent purposes of the Government towards them are faithfully fulfilled. No Liberian apprenticeship system is applicable to these Africans while in charge of the Society. Whatever may be said of the small sum (estimated even as low as ten dollars) at which a slave may somewhere be supported for a year, our Government has not, and we trust will not, put its humanity in question for the sake of economy, but continue to act towards these unfortunate victims of a most cruel commerce with a liberality due to their condition and its own character.

The Society has had sufficient experience to know that due provision cannot be made for the welfare of these Africans in Liberia (and in no other country can they be placed with so fair a prospect of civilization and happiness) for an expenditure less than has been in times past appropriated for their benefit.—*Nat. Intelligencer.*

## Latest from Liberia.

We have letters and papers from Liberia to the 21st of April. Mr. Dennis writes: "The last immigrants to Careysburg are doing well; none of them have died,—nearly all of them are now in their own houses. It is quite gratifying to our farmers to learn that the ship will bring out some sugar mills for sale."

## Receipts of the American Colonization Society,

*From the 20th of May to the 20th of June, 1860.*

### NEW HAMPSHIRE.

| | |
|---|---|
| By Rev. F. Butler, ($130,) viz: | |
| *Bristol*—Mrs. Almira Cavis and Miss H. M. Cavis, $5, S. Cavis, $3, Rev. Wm. S. Spalding, Wm. Green, C. Taylor, $1 each for the Arkansas people, | 11 00 |
| *New Hampton*—Col. Rufus G. Lewis, for the Arkansas people........................ | 20 00 |
| *Dover*—First Cong. Church and Society, to constitute their pastor, Rev. Elias H. Richardson, a life member.............. | 30 00 |
| *Exeter*—Mrs. J. Hurd, $2, Rev. J. Cole, $1................. | 3 00 |
| *West Lebanon*—Cong. Church & Society, $13, which, with previous donations, constitutes Rev. James Means a life member..................... | 13 00 |
| *Manchester*—Hon. G. W. Morrison, $4, Hon. W. C. Clarke, $3, Hon. S. Upton, P. K. Chandler, Mrs. Mace Moulton, $1 each................ | 10 00 |
| *Claremont*—Individuals......... | 4 00 |
| *Concord*—Custom Stearns, $10, Hon. M. Harvey, $5, J. B. Walker, $4, F. A. Fiske, S. Coffin, G. B. Chandler, $2 each, Benj. P. Stone, D. D., C. W. Flanders, D. D., Rev. H. E. Parker, A. Fletcher, James Moulton, jr., W. H. Allison, G. Hutchins, L. D. Stevens, R. Davis, Allen Tenney, S. G. Lane, Geo. Minot, Charles Minot, J. C. A. Wingate, $1 each,—whole to constitute Rev. C. W. Flanders, D. D., a life member........ | 39 00 |
| | 130 00 |

### CONNECTICUT.

| | |
|---|---|
| By Rev. John Orcutt ($254) viz: | |
| *New London*—Wm. C. Crump, Thomas W. Williams, each $20, A. M. Frink, A. Barnes, H. P. Haven, Mrs. M. H. Lewis, Mrs. S. Cleaveland, Mrs. Jona. Starr, Dr. W. W. Cutler, each $5, Mrs. S. R. Lockwood, $4, Miss E E. Rainey, Mrs. E. G. Gurley, Miss J. S Richards, Mrs. T. S. Chew, Mrs. Edward Learned, each $3, Cash, $1........ | 95 00 |
| *Greenwich*—Mrs. Sarah Mead, Miss Sarah Lewis, Mrs. Mary E. Mason, Augustus Mead, each $10, Lyman Mead, Isaac Lyon, each $5, Thomas A. Mead, $4, P. Button, Oliver Mead, Zaccheus Mead, each $3, Rev. Dr. Linsley, Mrs. Dr. Linsley, Rev. Mark Mead, Lot Mead, Joseph Brush, Edward Mead, Theo. Mead, J. A. Close, each $1........... | 71 00 |
| *Stamford*—E. Mosewood, J. Furgerson, Cash, Dea. Davenport, George Elder, Mrs. A. R. Starr, R. Swartwout, James Belts, each $5, Mrs. George Brown, $4, R. E. Rice, $3, Mrs. M. E. Rogers, $2....... | 49 00 |
| *Meriden*—Charles Parker, $20, J. & E. Parker, $10,—$30, to constitute their pastor, Rev. George A. Hubbell a life member; Gen. Walter Booth, $3.. | 33 00 |
| *New Haven*—Mrs. T. D. Wheeler........................ | 2 00 |
| *Hartford*—M. W. Chapin, $3, Ranson Reed, $1............ | 4 00 |
| | 254 00 |

NEW YORK.

By Rev. B O. Plimpton,($50.75) viz:

J. L. Heminger, $5, J. P. Dewey, $5, Wm. R. and Rebecca Wilson, $5, Hon. Joel Barnell, $5, J. Dewey, $2, Alfred Fife, $2, Sarah Shattuck, $5, R. P. Marvin, $2, Levi Burrows, $5, Daniel Hazleton, $3, W. H. Gifford, $2, Solomon Jones, $5, Mrs. Allen, $2, J. R Orten, $1, Reuben Orten, 50 cents, Ann Grigg, 25 cents, Caroline Ralph, 50 cents, Lydia W. Flower, 50 cents. (The residences not given by the Agent.) 50 75

PENNSYLVANIA.

By Rev. B. O. Plimpton,($61.25) viz:

N. C. Rogers, $2.50, A. M. Gray, $2.50, Geo. Barlow, $5, Joel Bradish, $5, Daniel Bear, $10, Samuel Myers, $1, Wm. Trimble, $10, Robert Morehead, $5, B. F. Beard, $5, A Friend, 25 cents, Elizabeth Devore, $5, Rev. Wm. Richins, and N G. Webber, $5 each—(Residences not given by the Agent)..................... 61 25

VIRGINIA.

*Piedmont Station*—Mrs. Judith Gibson, $1, "A Friend in Virginia," to constitute Mrs. Ann Trueheart, of Galveston, Texas, a life member of the A. C. S., $35........................ 36 00

OHIO.

By Rev. B. O. Plimpton,($55.75) viz:

L. Osbourn, $5, Rev. Mr. Nisbett, $8, Rev. John McKean, $10, Talcott Starr, $10, A. S. Plummer, $10, Samuel Northaid, $2.75, D. A Scott, $10.. 55 75

(*Note*—The residences not given by the Agent.)

WISCONSIN.

*Appleton*—Anson Ballard....... 1 00

MISSISSIPPI.

*Natchez*—Thomas Henderson... 200 00

LOUISIANA.

*Jackson*—John McKowan...... 100 00

---

FOR REPOSITORY.

MAINE.—*Augusta*—Edw'd. Rouse, 1 00

NEW HAMPSHIRE.—By Rev. F. Butler: *Bristol*—Hon. O. F. Fowler, $1, to May, '60, C. Taylor, $1, to Sept '60. *Sanbornton Bridge*—Asa P. Cate, $2, to May, '61. A H. Tilton, $3, to Oct. '61. *New Hampton*—Col. Rufus G Lewis, $5, for Rufus J D. Stewart and Rev. J. Fullerton, of New Hampton, Pastor of Cong. Church, Pastor of Methodist Church, Pastor F. W. Baptist Church of Bristol, to Oct. '60 *Dover*—Wm Woodman, $1, to Nov. '60. *Exeter*—Mrs. J. Hurd, $1, to Nov. '60. Mrs Mary Abbott, $2, to Nov. '59. Rev. J Cole, $1, to Nov. '60. *Nashua*—John A. Baldwin, $1, to Sept. '60. *West Lebanon*—Col. J. D. Hosley, $1, to July, '60. H. Nash, $1, to Sept. '60. *Lebanon*—Calvin Benton, $2, to July, '61. *Manchester*—P. Adams, $1 in full; Dr. J. Crosby, $1, to Oct. '60. J. Hersey, $1, to Oct. '60. Hon. G. W. Morrison, $1, to Jan. '60. Mrs. Mace Moulton, $1, to May, '61. *Claremont*—Jonas Livingston, $2, E. L. Goddard, $2, Jane Pierce, $2, each to Nov '60 *Concord*—J. B. Walker, $1, to Oct. '60—$34. *Mount Vernon*—F Kittredge, Jan. '59, to Jan. '61. $2...... 36 00

VERMONT.—*Charlotte*—Midas Prindle, Aug. '55, to Aug. '60. $5, Dr. John Strong, July, '59, to July, '61. $2................ 7 00

MASSACHUSETTS —*North Chester*—John S Cook, Jan. '58, to Jan. '61. $3. *Chester Factories*—H. L Lucas, $1.......... 4 00

CONNECTICUT —*New Haven*—Miss Mary Dutton, $1 *Meriden*—By Rev. John Orcutt, General Walter Booth, $1........... 2 00

NEW JERSEY.—*Trenton*—Miss Esther McIlvaine, in full, $5.. 5 00

PENNSYLVANIA.—*Lower Chanceford*—Matthew Wallace, in full, July, '55, to July, '60, $5. *Wellsborough*—Wm Bache, and J. F. Donaldson, each $1..... 7 00

OHIO.—By Rev. B. O. Plimpton: *Hudson*—William Dobbs, $1, in full...................... 1 00

MISSOURI.—*Kansas City*—Jackson Johnson, $1............... 1 00

| | |
|---|---|
| Total Repository........ | 64 00 |
| " Donations......... | 788 75 |
| Aggregate Amount...... | $852 75 |

## LIFE DIRECTORS.

Hon. THOS. W. WILLIAMS, Conn.,
THOMAS R. HAZARD, Esq., R. I.,
Rev. LEONARD BACON, D. D., Conn.,
Rev. EBENEZER BURGESS, D. D., Mass.,
FRANCIS GRIFFIN, Esq., Miss.,
Gen. JOHN H. COCKE, Virginia,
Rev. J. B. PINNEY, New York,
Rev. W. McLAIN, D. C.,
HERMAN CAMP, Esq., New York,
STEPHEN DUNCAN, M. D., Miss.,
JOHN MURDOCK, Esq., "
JAMES RAILEY, Esq., "
DAVID HUNT, Esq., "
NICHOLAS MILLS, Esq., Va.,
JAMES BOORMAN, Esq., N. Y.,
SOLOMON STURGES, Esq., Ohio,
HENRY STODDARD, Esq., "
Rev. JOHN MACLEAN, D. D., N. J.,
WILLIAM SILLIMAN, Esq., La.,
JAMES HALL, M. D., Md.,
Hon. MILLARD FILLMORE, N. Y.,
ALEXANDER DUNCAN, Esq., R. I.,
Hon. ALBERT FEARING, Mass.,
Rev. R. S. FINLEY, N. J.,
Hon. WILLIAM APPLETON, Mass.,
Rev. R. R. GURLEY, D. C.,
Hon. FRANKLIN PIERCE, N. H.,
GEORGE LAW, Esq., N. Y.,
Hon. EDWARD COLES, Pa.,
JOHN P. CROZER, Esq., Pa.
J. KNICKERBACKER, Esq., N. Y.,
DANIEL HUEY, Esq., Illinois.
CHARLES B. NEW, Esq., Miss.
Rev. JOHN ORCUTT, Conn.
Rev. JOSEPH TRACY, Mass.
Hon. WM. NASH, Vermont.

## Delegates appointed by State Auxiliary Societies for 1860.

MASSACHUSETTS—Hon. A. H. Rice.

CONNECTICUT—Hon. W. A. Buckingham, Hon. S. H. Huntington, Hon. J. A. Rockwell, General E. A. Elliott, Rev. R. J. Cone.

NEW YORK—Hon. D. S. Gregory, Caleb Swann, esq., Hon. Jas. W. Beekman, W. E. Dodge, esq., Hon. E. G. Spaulding, Smith Bloomfield, esq., Francis Hall, esq.

NEW JERSEY—Dr. L. A. Smith.

PENNSYLVANIA—William V. Pettit, esq., William Coppinger, esq.

OHIO—Hon. Thomas Corwin.

## *The Liberia Packet Ship Mary C. Stevens.*

THIS vessel was built with funds mainly derived from the late John Stevens, of Talbot County, Maryland, who voluntarily contributed $36,000 for this special purpose. Her ownership is vested in a Board of Trustees, but she is under the general direction of the Executive of the American Colonization Society. All charges of sailing and keeping the vessel in repair devolve upon the Society, and to it all proceeds and receipts for freight and passengers inure, and no other party is, in any way, interested in her earnings, or responsible for the liabilities she may incur.

She will sail regularly from Baltimore to Liberia, twice in each year, touching at all the ports twice in each voyage. Her regular days of sailing are, the 1st of May and 1st of November. She will take freight and passengers, to the extent of her capacity and accommodations, to and from Liberia, and from port to ports in Liberia. The American Colonization Society and its State Auxiliaries always to have the preference; next, emigrants going out in the ship; after which, in order of application.

TERMS OF FREIGHT AND PASSAGE.—Cabin Passage to any port in Liberia, or from any Liberia port to Baltimore, $100; Servants in the cabin, or children under ten years of age, half price, or $50; Steerage Passage either way, across the Atlantic, not paid by the Colonization Societies, $40; Children under ten years of age, half price, or $20; Cabin Passage, from any port in Liberia to the next nearest port, $5; For every additional port passed or touched at, $5; Steerage Passage on the Coast, half the above rates. Freight to be received and delivered alongside, or to be landed at risk and expense of consignees. Charges for landing or boating off cargo, 10 cents per bbl. and other cargo in proportion. For all freight over 5 bbls. in bulk, or 25 cubic feet, 30 cents per foot, or $1.50 per bbl. with primage accustomed. Camwood or metal, per ton, $10, with primage accustomed. Palm oil, per gallon, for capacity of casks, 5 cents, with primage accustomed. For all freight under 5 bbls. in bulk, 40 cents per foot, or $2 per bbl. No small packages, other than mailable matter, will be taken for less than $1. Letters and mailable matter, free of charge.

Freight consigned to irresponsible parties, or to non-residents of a port of entry, must invariably be paid in advance.

No freight will be received the two days previous to the sailing of the ship, that time being required for receiving on board provisions, emigrants and their effects.

*Directions to parties remote who have occasion to send Freight.*—Mark the packages plainly, with the person's name for whom they are intended, and place of residence, "care of Dr. James Hall, Colonization Office, Baltimore;" also enclose to him, by mail, at the time of sending a package, a receipt of the Carrier, with marks and numbers, whether by public or private conveyance. Freight to Baltimore, with necessary charges in the city, for drayage, porterage, wharfage, &c., must be added to the ship's freight out, as per above rates, and be paid by the shipper. Small sums may be remitted per mail in post office stamps.

Let it be remembered, that the only party interested in the ship is the American Colonization Society, whose funds are derived entirely from voluntary contributions, consequently no person or party, however charitable their object, can with propriety claim freight or passage gratuitously.

JAMES HALL, Agent.

---

## Terms of the Repository.

THE African Repository is issued regularly on the 1st of every month, at $1 per annum, *payable in advance.*

The Repository will be sent gratuitously—

To every clergymen who takes up annually a collection to aid the Am. Col. Society.

To every person who contributes annually ten dollars, or more, to the Society.

To every life member of the Society;—constituted by the payment of thirty dollars.

To every person obtaining three new subscribers, and remitting the money.

Subscribers who may not be visited by any of our regular agents, will please remit to the Financial Secretary and Treasurer of the Society, Washington, D. C., the amount of their subscription, in any kind of funds which may be most convenient to them; which will be acknowledged by mail, free of postage, and also in the succeeding number of the Repository.

Lightning Source UK Ltd.
Milton Keynes UK
UKHW010606120219
337137UK00007B/1560/P

9 780483 615366